Gumbo Circuitry:
Poetic Routes, Gastronomic Legacies

Andrew Jolivétte

Oklahoma City, Oklahoma
Calgary, Alberta
2024
[TPHP]

[The Geary Hobson & Ken Jolivétte Elder and Community Stories Series]

Gumbo Circuitry: Poetic Routes, Gastronomic Legacies

© 2024 by Andrew Jolivétte

ISBN 978-1-928708-15-5

Except for fair use in reviews and/or scholarly considerations, no part of this book may be reproduced, performed, recorded, or otherwise transmitted without the written consent of the author and the permission of the publisher.

Cover Art: "Throuple: Poly-Holy Trinity" © 2021 Rain Prud'homme-Cranford (FemnBelGrasArts)
Illustrations: © 2023 Rain Prud'homme-Cranford
Author photograph © 2013 Cecil Isidro
Introduction © 2024 Rain Prud'homme-Cranford and Andy Airey
Editor: Rain Prud'homme-Cranford
TPHP Editorial Assistant & TOC Layout: Noémie Foley
Assistant Proofing: Patrick Kuobâr Wayne with Carolyn Dunn
Book Design: That Painted Horse Press RPC
Cover Design: Rain Prud'homme-Cranford

That Painted Horse Press: A Borderless Press of the Americas
ThatPaintedHorsePress@gmail.com

Acknowledgements

With thanks to the editors of the following journals, books, and/or anthologies in which these poems, sometimes in different forms or titles, have appeared:

"Revolution, "*Obama and the Biracial Factor*, Bristol University Press, 2012.

Hiwéwéw (Much Thanks)

First, I want to acknowledge my mother Annetta and my father Kenneth who were my first and my best teachers. You both instilled love and joy in my heart and taught me to care for my community while sharing all that I could. I hope I make you proud and I hope you'd be thrilled with this book of poems and recipes for dishes you both inspired. Next, I want to thank my grandmothers, Gertie Lee Fontenot and Isabella Americus Hicks, both remarkable women who taught me so much, especially my paternal grandmother Gertie who owned and operated her own restaurant in San Francisco. I want to give so much love to my sisters, the editorial dream team that made this work possible—Drs. Rain Prud'homme-Cranford and Carolyn Dunn. You and our cousins/kin folks, Darryl, Jeff, Tracey, Maaliyah, Robert, Jean-Luc, Joseph, and so many others make this ceremonial dreamwork all the more beautiful. To our tribal chair, Chief Edward Chretien and to our council members (especially our elders and knowledge keepers), my most sincere thanks— Hiwéw/ Mési. To my cousin and friend of 30 years, Felicia Gustin, mil gracias for the idea of putting my love for words and food together in the form of a poetry cookbook. To my colleagues at UC San Diego in the Ethnic Studies Department and beyond, my gratitude for your support and encouragement over the past four and a half years and especially as I worked on this project. Our stories are never just our own. They are reflections of our ancestors, of our dream spaces, of the places where love makes us feel whole and complete. To my loving husband, Anthony Marte...You complete me in so many ways. Your support, love, and encouragement make this work possible in ways I did not imagine. Sharing our lives is a true gift. Your own talent as a chef and as a humanbeing are my daily inspiration. I love you endlessly. Finally, to my aunts Greta, Stephanie, Karen, and Sheila, my uncle and Godfather, Charlie Jolivétte and to my niece Anaya and my godchildren, Dinari and Nassima...thank you for being my family and for holding the legacies of our ancestors together—you along with Mama Janet Ravare Colson and Terrel Delphin have been my constant sources of strength.
 ~Wi hokišak kuš (We Are All Relations/Connected)~

Ingredients

Dedication
Preface
Introduction: "Kekfwa vou planté zariko rouj. Zariko blan ki pousé "....i
Forward: The Net..ix

I. Séléri: Breakfast in the Bayou
Water from Mother..2
That Creole Smile..5
For Creole Love...7
Traces..9
Ruptures..10
Standing Together 12
A Poem for Elgin...14
Revolution...15

Recipes
Seafood Gumbo...19
Baked Salmon with Shrimp, Chorizo, White Wine Sauce 21
Green Curry and Basil Coconut Ribs...23
Camarones a la Diabla 24
Smothered Okra with Chicken, Sausage and Shrimp........................25
Caribbean Basa with Coconut Mint and Orange Cream Sauce.............27

II. Hatoflvha: Lunch in Louisiana
Black Futurity, Black Joy 30
COVID-19 AKA Coronoavirus 33
COVID Response 36
Rez-Erect Me..38
Was it August or October? 41
Hyphy 44

Recipes
Andrew's Opelousas-Cali Sausage, Chicken and Shrimp Jambalaya
Topped with Fried Catfish and Crab Legs 51
Shrimp, Crab, and Crawfish Étouffée..53
Garlic & Butter Roasted Chicken Stuffed with a Shrimp, Crab, and Bacon
Dressing..54
Ribeye Steak and Mango Salsa Frybread Sliders 56
Pork Belly Mac and Cheese..57
Roasted Pork Tenderloin in a Blackberry Pear Sauce over Spinach, Blue
Cheese, and Bacon Salad..59

III. Pimen Dou: Dinner and Dancin
Give it All to the People...62
In God's Own Image..64
Enraptured...66
You Compliment Me...68
Not One Word...71
A Thousand Times...72
JCB..73
Thrivance...76

Recipes
Creole Stuffed Chile Relleno Peppers..81
Baked Cushaw (Squash)...83
Crab and Lobster Bisque..84
Crawfish, Sausage, Shrimp, and Crab Fettucine..............................85
Andrew's Shrimp & Beef Burgers...87
Creole Seafood Stuffed Red Snapper with a Jalapeno Chimichurri Sauce..89

IV. Lagniappe: Evening Conaque in Cali
Gumbo Circuitry..93
Afterword: Hiwéw Shokmiso Hoktiwé..97
About the Author...99
Contributors..101

Dedication

For my father, my daddy, Kenneth Louis Jolivétte, Sr.
(December 11th, 1949-March 16th, 2022)

My daddy, who taught me joy, laughter, and cooking
I love you always,
Chér Baby

Preface

This book is an invitation into the poetic routes and gastronomic legacies of Louisiana Creole, Latin American, Native American, West African, and Caribbean influenced culinary arts as well as original creative writings, that for me are oft some of the most pressing social, political, and cultural themes of the 21st century. *Gumbo Circuitry,* through poetic and culinary arts, documents various movements and fusions of cultures, histories, and contestations of Louisiana Creole, Indigenous, African, and Latinx peoples across Turtle Island and globally. As one of the first Creole-Indigenous books to fuse the circuits of Creole Culinary arts with poetry (joining such works as Rain Prud'homme's *Smoked Mullet Cornbread Crawdad Memory* [2012] and Therese Style's children's collection *The Creole and the Caterpillar: A book of poetry, Creole recipes, love and Louisiana culture,* [2016]); it is a project of remembrance and thrivance. Thrivance is the active assertion of one's everyday practices as sites of not only survival and resistance, but more importantly of joy, knowledge creation, and self-determination. This work is the culmination of centuries of memories of racialized peoples who traversed many routes and legacies in the formation of contemporary identity in Indigenous, Black, and Latinx communities. The hands of my mother, grandmother, and aunts are the backbone of this project. While these recipes are a mixture of various traditions and bring new methods and practices to the culinary arts — it is also significant that the work engages and recuperates Louisiana and Gulf Creole cooking as an on-going highly consumed genre that contests simple reduction to any one area or anyone population. The poems were written in response to moments of crisis, healing, foreclosures, and resistances. Food and poetry are inherently about resistance, about self-determination. The art and tradition that bore what follows stems from a long line of matriarchs, and yes patriarchs, who used ingredients available to them from the land Indigenous to them, creating an explosive range of dishes centering techniques that were not only about food preparation but also about family and community gatherings. Food in the context of this project represents what I term 'Kin-Gatherings.' This book is fundamentally about shifting narratives of cultural resilience to cultural thrivance. How do our words, our forms of nourishment lead to community thrivance? By centering our own cultural and traditional knowledge systems we are changing the ways that we understand society and the changing face of the United States and the world.

~ Andrew Jolivétte, Ah-ha Kwe-ah-mac (San Diego), 2023

An Introduction in Call and Response
"Kekfwa vou planté zariko rouj. Zariko blan ki pousé."

Rain:
There is an old Louisiana Creole[1] saying, "kekfwa vou planté zariko rouj. Zariko blan ki pousé," meaning literally, "sometimes you plant red beans and white beans grow." In other words, things don't always go as planned, or wind up, or even look, as expected. The work of celebrated sociologist and Louisiana Creole/Ishak Indigenous rights activist Andrew Jolivétte brings this phrase to mind. Our culture and genes as Creoles are a literal gumbo: African, Native American, European, Caribbean. Defying constructs of "race" Louisiana Creoles are a culture—a Peoplehood. We "sprout" in a rainbow of colors with an array of talents. It is these talents, that those most familiar with Jolivétte's work as an academic, will be most surprised. This collection is part memorial, part celebration, part "calling in" (as opposed to calling out), and part carnivale. But more than anything, this collection is a love letter to Louisiana's Creole, Native American, and Latinidad communities, in other words, a love letter to Indigenous Louisiana, in the homeland and the diaspora. This is a multimodal story that starts and ends with feasting. While not Dr. Jolivétte's first book, this is his first (debut) poetry and cookbook collection, where food is land. Food is family. And in this creative and cultural collection Jolivétte celebrates the intimacies of kinship and story as it rises from land into the food we cook, to the stories we tell at our dinner tables, and songs we sing on front porches sipping chicory coffee—listening as the Spanish moss whispers a Creole lullaby.

As both an academic and artist, Jolivétte's positionality also speaks to representation. I know personally what it means to see Creole Indigeneity and queerness represented alongside our culture, landbases, stories, and ancestors. But as an educator, I also have seen firsthand the ways in which Jolivétte's humanity and openness has impacted students, Native, Black, Latinx, and even settlers, as well as other marginalized queer/non-binary/trans* artists and thinkers. And as such, this collection has many stories, and those stories surely impact and change through the corpus of the reader.

---

[1] When referring to Creoles we use Louisiana Creole to encompass the Afro-Indigenous culturally grounded people belonging to the lands of Louisiana.

Andy:
I first encountered Dr. Jolivétte's work in a methodologies class on Indigenous and Afro-Indigenous onto-epistemologies, taught by Dr. Prud'homme-Cranford in 2022. As a settler student of Celtic and Norse origins (and as such distant Sámi ancestry), I had enrolled in university on a personal journey towards reconciliation. Adrift from the constructions of Canadian state identity, I longed for intrinsic culture, to know what right I had to love the land that supported me even so far from the ancestral homes that made my bones ache with longing. Coming face-to-face with my unsettled-ness, I was desperate for healing. I continue to seek reconciliation between myself and the land I occupy, while addressing the colonial fragmentation that has resulted in the construction of my own whiteness, precipitating and perpetuating cycles of harm.

During the term with Dr. Prud'homme-Cranford we were assigned an interview with Dr. Jolivétte on "Equity Talks." I was captured by his ideas of "radical love" and "thrivance." As Jolivette explains: "To thrive or enact thrivance means to turn our traumas and vulnerabilities into moments and possibilities to change our lives."[2] From there we were introduced to his application of radical love (expanded from Patrick Chang) in which "radical love challenges the social boundaries that suggest that certain types of love (queer love, Indigenous love, interracial love) are less valid than other types of loving relationships. Moreover, radical love asks us to take personal responsibility for the well-being of those who are most different from us."[3] Why was it that whenever I witnessed Black and Indigenous resistance and reclamation that I felt such primordial resonance? Like tremors along the fault lines of my own colonial constructions that made me want to jump up and shout, "That! That!"

I felt it when I heard Dr. Jolivette that day, and whenever I read his work thereafter. What resonated is Jolivétte's planting of ancient feet in the earth amidst a crowd of ancestors visible and more-than, extending a palm of vulnerability. A lived model for healing, bridging, and the

---

[2] Jolivétte, Andrew. "What's Pride Got to Do with It? Black and Indigenous Erasure in HIV and Public Health." *San Francisco AIDS Foundation*, 4 Mar. 2021.

[3] Jolivétte, Andrew. *Indian Blood: HIV and Colonial Trauma in San Francisco's Two-Spirit Community*. University of Washington Press, 2016.

lifetime work of being a good relation. And in doing so, offering settlers like me a better map, and better way to be *in* relation while working towards mending my own compliances in the colonial mission and healing toward my own reclamation of Celt and Norse ancestors.

Lés-yé parlé (Let them talk)

Rain:
On more than one occasion I have witnessed the way Andrew's applications of radical love and thrivance have resonated and impacted students and members of Afro-Indigenous communities alike, along with other marginalized folx, and settler allies. I have been blessed to give talks and discussion tables with Andrew and other Creole, Indigenous, Afro-Indigenous thinker-scholar-artist-activists as we remind folx: Louisiana Creoles are Indigenous; Black folx are Indigenous; Latinx folx are Indigenous. While also asserting: Yes! Sovereignty matters. Thus, being good kin for Louisiana Creoles is also upholding sovereignty, even as Creoles struggle for autonomy and voice themselves. Yes there are histories of access, class, colorism, lateral violence, politics, factions, and anti-Black racism. As a güera Kréyol femn gra, cis-queer, fat Louisiana Creole I also move in the world with a privilege not extended to my melanated kinfolx. I and others have witnessed Dr. Jolivétte be attacked with internalized settler colonial lateral violences, including being called a "field n*" by a public-facing researcher and other derogatory epitaphs on social media platforms, often fueled by anti-Blackness[4]— All of which erase Louisiana Creole culture through white/black binaries. Part of purging the infection of settler colonialism is in speaking lived truth, and so Jolivétte speaks his truth, daring his critics and anti-Black factions with the Kouri Vini adage: Lés-yé parlé (Let them talk). Many of us in Louisiana communities have been exposed to the very real limitations of colonial archives of "documentation" against oral narratives and lived culture/embodied cultural practice when addressing Afro-Indigeneity/Afro-Indigenous culture, and the very real threat of misinformation and miseducation informed by systemic anti-Blackness and legacies of passé blanc survivals in the South. As playwright-poet-scholar-educator Carolyn Dunn writes:

---

[4] Recent animosities directed to tribal communities of the Houma and Lumbee, for example, have also been attributed to Anti-Blackness.

This is what bothers me specific to Louisiana Indigenous peoples because of the racialized mixing that has been going on since Louisiana first became colonized. This is also an issue because this happens in other states but specifically to Louisiana because of mixing and creating a _completely new post-contact Afro-Indigenous culture_ from the strands of *all three of its parent cultures*: Indigenous peoples of Turtle Island and Africa, as well as settlers (Europeans). We continue to struggle against anti-Black racism and Indigenous erasure. Moreover, the records, historic, oral, material, etc are complex, and those not well-trained in the area are oft more likely to perpetuate erasure and settler myths around Louisiana Creole identity and Afro-Indigenous culture.[5]

But as Andy reminds us, Andrew centers thrivance through the ability to transform trauma into thriving joy and artivism (art as activism). Thus, as Jolivétte writes in the preface that while this collection is "written in response to moments of crisis, healing, foreclosures, and resistances. Food and poetry are inherently about resistance, about self-determination…" where the poems and food are "fundamentally about shifting narratives of cultural resilience to cultural thrivance… By centering our own cultural and traditional knowledge systems we are changing the ways that we understand society and the changing face of the United States and the world." *Gumbo Circuitry* does just this, centering Louisiana Creole practices and thrivance turning traumas of colonial violences, Indigenous erasure, and anti-Black racism into artivism where

>We begin again
>We thrive.
>We thrive.
>We thrive.

In the poem "Thrivance" Jolivétte articulates a clear sense of community across generations intimately connected to land through removal, violence, and diaspora while resolutely *here. Present.* Practicing a rooted culture older than America — birthed from this soil before America was "America." Conjuring the smells and sounds of the boucherie Jolivétte writes:

---

[5] Prud'homme-Cranford, Rain and Carolyn M Dunn. "'Shell shaking sisters and chain cries blues': Creole Tidalectics & Echolocative Indigenous Rhetorical Praxis." *Native American Poets Doing Theory, Methodology, Pedagogy.* Eds. Inés Hernández-Ávila and Molly McGlennen. Michigan State University Press, East Lansing MI –2024 forthcoming–

Remember
our birthplace,
our land,
our water
our songs.

So, we sing again.
We stomp our feet on the ground.
Where Nanan stopped bleeding with her medicines.

We stomp our feet where Pop fed the people.
The cotton fills the quilts and the crawfish
still float to the top when we flood them out.

Creation begins with
all our relations.
So, we stomp
and we live.

These poems, these recipes, are more than re-rememberings. They are embodied living, adapting, and fertile— They are constelled stories and feasts with which to sing ourselves and our ancestors' home— continuously, through histories of violence, erasures, assimilations (attempted and successful), and political paper genocides— manifesting in the will, resistance, resilience, and unadulterated joy of being *Creole Rooted*.

Andy:
In the poem "Rez-Erect Me," Andrew pops the blister around Black/Black-Indian/Creole and queer bodies, where objectification makes a thin membrane of safety until it doesn't.
   Your teardops burn holes in sunlit flesh…

   Your pale skin
   Your weak emotional capacity
   Your sheep in wolves clothing
   Those dirty knees lost smells of innocence generations ago

Juxtaposing the "sunlit flesh" of natural queerness with the foul of privileged pale normativity, the poem oozes disgust of hypocrisy, all the while baring its teeth – *I am not your Red-Black meat*! As a surgically affirmed transgender individual, it took a scalpel to make me whole, seaming the split of my two selves—a young man and a crone. Yet even with their combined gifts, I still don't know what to do when a stranger pushes their hand down the crevice of my novelty.

Still, white cocks have leverage, even at the margins. As Andrew writes
> You wreak of privilege
> even when you bow down
> Mouth Wide Open...
> Begging for red cocks to begin new days

Thus, this poem reminds me in no uncertain shades just how much my experience turns sallow in the shadow of centuries of colonial occupation, where the ecological sacredness of IBPOC queer bodies was put up for contract, to be extracted or expunged at the discretion of its settler objectifiers. In this sense, the poem spares no punches in its exposure of lived realities as a Louisiana Creole-Indigenous Two-Spirit/Queer. Stating his truth, he proclaims: "Let them talk!"

Kalibas-la swiv lalyán (The gourd follows the vine)

Rain:

Food works as the proverbial vine connecting us to both the land from which we ourselves and that which gives us sustenance emerge. It is the vine we oft travel as a way to access memory: Dad and Nanan cooking in the kitchen. Mawmaws and Aunties snapping beans on the porch telling stories of those who have walked on. This food, which grows from mother, also carries the memories and remains of our ancestors whose bones return to these very soils. And so, through food Jolivétte accesses cultural memory creating tables of spiritual and physical sustenance. Organized through the holy trinity: bell peppers, onions, and celery, with lagniappe (a little extra), while highlighting languages Indigenous to Louisiana, of which Kouri Vini (Louisiana Creole) belongs— The recipes explore both Creole rootedness and Louisiana Creoles in the diaspora. For me, none exhibits this as deftly as his "Creole Stuffed Chile Relleno Peppers." Like the Creole classic stuffed mirlitons, the stuffing echoing the Creole flavors of home while encased in the sweet heat of poblano peppers and cheese, like a chile relleno. This recipe is a feast of flavor where Creole zydeco meets Mexicana banda, and like two partners dancing the bamboula, boy does it drum soulful flavor on tastebuds!

Andy:

In my previous life as a classical singer, I was absurdly fortunate to travel around the world, even in my teens under the colonial gilding of "white excellence." Andrew's recipe, "Green Curry and Basil Coconut Ribs" makes me think of when, at seventeen, I was invited to sing in Bangkok, Thailand. Here, I had my first taste of green curry. It shocked me. Bright and rich and alien and full of context. *So this was what culture tasted like*. The talk, heart, longing of a people all crowded onto my tongue. But I had no words for it then, nothing but overwhelm in my boxed, 2-minute conglomerate palate; a watery broth of belonging to the word 'Canadian.' Jolivétte merges flavors as a Creole in diaspora, working alongside other peoples and cultures through culinary translations of radical love. This vine flows always returning home to the gourd of Louisiana.

Tawhatwén'nto Ocotātot (I stand praying to God)

Andy:
"Water From Mother" is an echolocative entry into *Gumbo Circuitry* reminding me exactly why I fell in love with Andrew's work in the first place. The tender power of his opening refrain, rising and retreating, lapping: "Water from Mother/ ancient places of knowing… Water from Mother/ a temple resting reposed… Water from Mother/ Enter house of ancient songs." For me—at ancient spaces of longing tucked into the saline of my cells— this poem reverberates. There is a truly oceanic power in never having to say, "this is *my* mother," but in letting it be witnessed. Through intimacy, through history, through tragedy, in this poem Andrew reveals his umbilical selfhood in quiet spaces behind words, like foam settling after the waves. Rejecting the English language trap of ownership, Jolivétte belongs himself to the land, teaching and reminding people like me— that somewhere, deep in blood memory, I know that feeling too. The rock-and-forth of ancestral seas whispering "you're home. You're home. In these waters you're home." If my own longing and grief for my long-lost cultures can model anything, I hope it's for the vital celebration and protection of works like these. Where food is sovereignty, from land to belly and soul. A declaration to the state, to norms, to hegemony: "taste this, and tell me I don't know exactly who the fuck I am."

Rain:
This collection is a love letter to Louisiana's Creole, Native American, and Latinidad communities. A love letter to Indigenous Louisiana, in the

homeland and the diaspora. This is evident in the ways community has come together giving thanks to Andrew for his role in keeping the elder fires burning. From the opening poem of thanks by Tracey Colson-Antee, who memorializes Andrew and our generations' journey into taking up the call of elders who have passed, to the closing hatwén (prayer) written in Ishakkoy, by Maaliyah Papillion— a young rising leader of the Atakapa-Ishak Nation of southwest Louisiana. One of my favorite poems in the book was not originally part of the collection. It came into being through annexation and reinvention, pulling strands from disparate parts singing a song of both love and resistance. In "For Creole Love" Jolivétte traces delicate vines of eco-erotic intimacies of land-kin to the embodied erotic of falling-in and making love:

> Lay in this field with me
> embraced under Louisiana turquoise sky
> Fall with me into the
> bayou pools of each other's eyes

> *Come trail ride with me*
> *Come let's LaLa once more*
> *la joie de vivre*

The refrain, "*Come trail ride with me/ Come let's LaLa once more/ la joie de vivre*" ebbs and flows a tidal guide to carry us back to the homeland, so we might "zydeco…back under Louisiana Skies."

It takes sure soles rooting strong souls to know oneself. This collection sings from that place of sureness, guided by memory, family, land, and prayer. This collection has been a long time coming. From its first inception through various iterations, we have loved, lost beloved elders, battled illness, and watched as another genocide unfolds. There is a reason Indigenous people of Turtle Island stand in solidarity with Palestine. We recognize that love of kin, homeland, and the struggle to exist in a world seeking to erase us. And as a Creole-Ishak, Jolivétte calls upon that love like a prayer for healing. So, beside Andrew and our all relations, tawhatwén'nto ocotātot. And I give thanks… *for this Creole Love.*

~Rain Prud'homme-Cranford,
Chassahowitzka
~Andy Airey,
Mohkínstsis
2024

The Net

~For brother Andrew

He weaves the net
pulling from earth, moss, and leaves
creating vibrant color where all was gray

Slowly, over decades the net grows
It gains color, multiplying, deep pigmented earth
worked and reworked by hands aged and youthful

Textures mesh from the ancestral home,
soft cotton and worn leather to rough braids
made with Spanish moss and scattered thorns

He weaves the net
It looks like family, of blood, and of love
Feels like sunlit warm strength wrapped around you

The net catches me when I fall
Lifts me up, covers me, and cradles me
strong, sustaining, and reaching over land and ocean

His net
fills the empty spaces
envelopes me, envelopes us all
For he has weaved it with all the pieces of who we are

This net is solid and sturdy
It is the place I land, stopping the fall
He weaves the net in unending love,
with peace and power woven for us all

~Tracey Colson-Antee
Opelousas
2024

I. Séléri: Breakfast in the Bayou

Water from Mother
- for my mother, Annetta Donan Foster Jolivétte

I.
Water from Mother
like waves kissing white sand
on summer horizon
stained in red warmth of rising sun

Water from Mother
ancient places of knowing
and unknowing in dawns of disaster
where dew drops trickle triumph

Water from Mother
tears of unchained slaughters
from silences and remains
to dust and disrepair

Water from Mother
a temple resting reposed
at feet of God's rising and flowing
like Birds Paradise to settle
in the aches and arches of my back

Re-birth me, Re-birth us
Re-birth this taste, rebirth this smell
Water from Mother's Womb

II.
Water from Mother's Womb
recoil from empty gray earth
Recoil and Remember
Remember
Remember

Re-Birth — passing moments
this death unearthing site
Mother offers miraculous excavations
resurrections where love once stood

Mother's Tears water
dancing upon my dry flaking dead skin
unmasking lye-stained settler stench
slapping back each hand that takes, takes, takes
without pause or haste

Mother's Tears water heating hard, cold carved stone
washing rivulets of rebirth over forgotten
unseen rose quartz stone beats to water and sunlight

Rainbows bring forgiving,
Rainbows in halos of light bring rebirth
Rainbows' memory calls back awakens days gone

III.
Water from Mother
Enter house of ancient songs,
sing a chorus over
discord, sorrow, and weeping
Sung day and night
Sing a chorus silencing
screams and bitterness

Water from Mother
Open your navel once more,
gather all wounds of all children
Open arms of all Mothers,
held in arms of Ancient Ones

When this world is crumbling
shifting below upon too
mined plates of coal and ash,
and sunken drained aquifers

Let Water
from Mothers
Flood Down
Flood Down
Flood Down

becoming waterfalls
of purple corn
feeding a Generation

> *Thirsty for the mercy of your hand in uncovered light*

That Creole Smile
For the one with those old-world Guillory eyes that make me smile

Lurking—
Shimmering—
Shining around every bend of river

There at sunlight's rise
There—
at moonlight's peak
that Creole Smile

> So far, yet so close
> there's my beau
> there's my destiny
> there's my chér joli

There's that Creole smile

Smiling sing songs from
churches to bayous
Whisper me a story
Grin that smile, only you can
Turn on the porch light
Viens ici

And just show me,
show me that old Creole smile

Heal Me,
Heal Us,
Heal All
Broken Hearts

Unfork crooked tongues turn
into French Creole laughter,
laughter and love
Smiling in the light

> So far, yet so close
> there's my beau

          there's my destiny
          there's my chér joli

There is no beauty,
There is no laughter,
There is no smile

No not one
Not one
Not one
Not a one

Flesh of my father's flesh
Breath of my
Grandmother's Grandmother

Not any like that old Creole smile

For Creole Love
"Les cenelles. Ye repousse/ Ferme et beau, comme/ notre fidele, amour Creole."
~ Armand Lanusse ("Pour Ulysse Richard")

We begin
We enter
We become

As wind breaks through Louisiana sky
I fall into arms of ancestors
into a love that's always been waiting

> *Come trail ride with me*
> *Come let's LaLa once more*
> *la joie de vivre*

In the field on horseback
engulfed by humidity
scents of horses and grass abound

Lay in this field with me
embraced under Louisiana turquoise sky
Fall with me into the
bayou pools of each other's eyes

> *Come trail ride with me*
> *Come let's LaLa once more*
> *la joie de vivre*

You are my gift
and I am yours
Take my hand come
sing songs by rivers

Black cast iron skillets filled to brim
Come sip the gumbo from my lip
Taste the lagniappe in my soul

> *Come trail ride with me*
> *Come let's LaLa once more*
> *la joie de vivre*

One in a long line of Creole lovers,
sitting with me beneath fig trees
sunbeams across your face
Eat couche couche and grattons

These hearts that burn
with ancient passions,
beating like stomped boots

> *Come trail ride with me*
> *Come let's LaLa once more*
> *la joie de vivre*

Boots tapping upon wood floors
Les haricots sont pas sales!
Let's Zydeco! Let's Zydeco!
Hei Toi! Hei Toi!

And zydeco me back
under Louisiana skies
grab your father's bridle
bring your mother's map
and…

> *Come trail ride with me*
> *Come let's LaLa once more*
> *la joie de vivre*

Traces

In absence of your presence
I submit to physical traces of your memory.
In wonderment that is the unknown I succumb
once more to the intimate spaces between us.

Today I hold forever in my heart.
No words need be exchanged...
just the sighting of your face and the scent
of your warmth halts earth.

Your wit and intellect penetrate my wandering rushed mind.

I give to you my patience.
I present to you my open arms
where home is always waiting...

Where doing is living.
And where living is loving.

Ruptures

Ripped from earth's red skin
pinched, pulled, stretched out against time—
Ruptures create soul wounds
across thousands of nations.

Dissolved centers, softening like wet cotton
scars slowly staining, slowly soaking—
ghosts haunt as we sleep— As we wake.

No place for memory to hide—
No place for memory to resolve, to resist—
We are haunted, we are broken bone and ash.
We are ancient mounds desecrated,

under grandfather ceremonial rocks lies
contaminated waters, underground pollution
from frack, extract, and drill.

Yet remember, here in the cracks
of earth we emerged out of wombs of
dead mothers, where pale faced ghosts
affix themselves to our children.
These colonial hauntings make us living haints.

Gone in the sun of a thousand dancers,
our spirit traumas remain.
Invasion syndrome re-triggers
every trauma— every act of settler violence.

Yet, here in this new morning light
beneath Spanish moss and eucalyptus
among smells of venison, salmon, and
cowan. We begin a new fire
so, our people can eat—
so, our people can dance—

We are Two-Spirit.
We are "between."

Two-Spirit dissolved,
Two-Spirit names:
Wíŋkte, Nádleehi, lhamana, changing ones —

Dance a dance only our
grandmothers' feet recognize —
> We begin again
> We sing again
> We gather again
> We restore ancestor memory.

In ceremony we wipe frozen tears.
In ceremony we re-stitch ruptured bodies.
In ceremony we return to our knowledge systems,
unmasking our truths in multi-colored blankets and shawls
exchanging skin, blood, and radical love —
Our vulnerability is key to becoming re-born.

Returning we reach out
whispering to the sacred
We hear. We remember.
We remain. We rupture no more.
We are dissolved no longer.

We revoke every haunting,
every rape, every unsober moment.
We sing a return to the sacred.
Looking to moon I feel consecrated blessings,
and in the undilated pupils of our sisters and brothers.

Look to the elders. Turn to the youth.
You are your own healing.
Be your own Truth.
This is our best medicine.

Dance a dance only our
grandmothers' feet recognize —
> We begin again
> We sing again
> We gather again
> We restore ancestor memory.

Standing Together

Stand Your Ground —
You there, the son of the Black man
son of the poet,
daughter of the Frenchman.
Stand your ground.

You there —

brother to the Filipino,
teacher of the Tongan,
friend of the Salvadoreno...

Stand your ground making seeds grow,
from nothing we make
seeds grow —

Light-up dusty dark streets
dancing feet on land ancestors stood.
Light Fires to warm hearts.
Light Fires to speak truth.
Light Fires for generations to see.

You there —

the student,
the teacher —
look across time and hear their voices —

> "We believe in you,
> we believe in you —
> we believe in you.
>
> Stand your ground.
> Stand your ground.
> Stand your ground."

Open your books and let the brilliance of the light shine.
Let the brilliance from your soul shine.
Let All Futures be Yours.

You are dreams of ancestors re-born.
You will be the teacher, the doctor,
the senator, the professor, the artist
we are waiting for you.

We are standing ground with you —

YOU ARE HERE
WE ARE HERE
SPIRIT IS HERE

On this ground,
on this day together...
We Are Stronger!

A Poem for Elgin

Give me your Black body, give me your pain
Give me your tears, give me your sorrow—
      But Keep Your Spirit for yourself

Give me your anguish, give me your hurt
Give me your despair, give me your wounds—
      But keep your laughter for yourself

Give me the faggots, give me the queers
Give me the false gazes, give me the fears—
      But keep your smile for yourself

Give me a thousand years of their doubts
Give me a thousand words of regret
give me your death—
So I can wipe away the tears

But Keep Your Heart
Keep Your Truth
Keep You…
For Yourself

      Sleep Well Dear Elgin.

Revolution

There was something sleeping within me
and there you were to awaken it.
There was this silence unexposed
that you broke through shattering a million fragmented
pieces into a new whole.

When I had forgotten who I was,
you were there to restore
what was hidden deep within.

There was something sleeping within me
and there you were to awaken it
reminding me what it means to laugh.
Reminding me what it means to be free and true.

There was this silence unexposed
that you broke through.
With your smile, your unhidden expression filled.
You reminded me the power of wind
to create breath, the power of
wind to allow life to breathe in its full and complete joy
revealing new experiences unknown.

Revolution isn't a place.
Revolution isn't a person.
Revolution is the fruit of desire.

Revolution is:
community
connections
spaces
relationships

Awake to revolution.
It is strong and free.
It is alive within you…
It is alive within me.

Even with the absence of your touch,

of your lips against my skin, this memory is
a reminder of the revolution within.

There was something sleeping within me
and there you were to awaken it.
Quietly, gently you allowed me
to be me. Us to be us. Unmasked in
the warmth of a revolutionary sun.

This fire burns...
and bares our revolution.
A Revolution born from
a seed planted for our own.

We grow a REVOLUTION!

RECIPES

Seafood Gumbo

Ingredients:
1 Cup of All-Purpose Flour
1 Cup of Vegetable Oil
1 Red Bell Pepper
1 Green Bell Pepper
1 Yellow Bell Pepper
1 Yellow Onion
64 oz of Chicken Broth
32 oz of Seafood Broth
2 Bunches of Green Onions
6-10 Bay Leaves
1 Package of Dried (Shell Free) Baby Shrimp
Creole Seasoning 1/4 Cup
Garlic Powder 1/3 Cup
3-4 Tablespoons of Shrimp/Seafood Boil (Optional)
3 LBS of Sausage (1LB Smoked, 1LB Andouille, 1LB Italian)
2 LBS of Boneless Chicken Breast or Thigh Meat
2LBS of Peeled and Deveined Shrimp
3 Jars of Oysters
4 Snow Crab Clusters
1 16 oz Can of Claw Crab Meat
3-4 Tablespoons of Gumbo Filé

Methods:
Heat oil in 20-quart stock pot and add flour and seasoning and stir

rigorously until the roux becomes a dark chocolate color. Be careful not to let your roux sit without stirring as it may burn. Once your roux is done add the chopped vegetables which will slow the cooking process and mix well.

Add chicken and seafood broth. If you can't find seafood stock, you can make your own by removing the shells from the shrimp and boiling them in 4 cups of water with Creole seasoning. Strain and remove the shells and add the shrimp broth to your pot bringing to a boil. Add more seasoning to your pot.

For those who desire a smoky gumbo you may add smoked neckbones to your gumbo. Let the gumbo cook for about 30-45 minutes. In the meantime, boil your sausage and lightly brown your chicken by seasoning and frying in oil (do not add flour to the chicken when browning). Once your sausage is cooked let it cool then slice into ¼ inch pieces. Add the chicken and sausage to your gumbo and let it cook for another 30-45 minutes tasting occasionally to see if you want to add more seasoning.

At this point you can add the seafood boil for additional spice and flavoring. If your gumbo seems too thick just add more broth. It will continue to thicken as you cook it. After a total of about $1^{1/2}$ to 2 hours of total cook time you may add your shrimp, crab, and oysters to the pot. Let this cook for another 15-20 minutes. Remove 3-4 cups of the gumbo and add to a large bowl and whisk in the file to taste and then return to the pot and add bay leaves, chopped green onions, and dried shrimp to the pot and stir well. Let this cook maybe 10 more minutes then turn off. Serve over rice.

Baked Salmon with Shrimp, Chorizo, and White Wine Sauce

Ingredients:

2-4 Pieces of Skinless Atlantic Salmon Fillets
1/2 pound of peeled and deveined shrimp (you may choose to use up to 1lb)
1/2 pound of , chorizo or soy chorizo or fresh ground pork or beef
1 bunch of green onions
1 bunch of fresh parsley
4 finely diced cloves of garlic
1 cup of white wine (Chardonnay would be best)
Creole Seasoning
Garlic Powder
1/2 Cup of water
1 lemon
1 large white or yellow onion chopped and diced
1 to 2 teaspoons of sugar
1 stick of butter

Method:

In a 13 x 9 deep dish baking pan add just enough water to the bottom of the pan so there is water across the pan. Add to the pan the salmon pieces and season on both sides with Creole seasoning and garlic powder. Bake in the oven on 350° for about 15-20 minutes. In a large skillet melt one stick of butter and add chopped onion and garlic until the onions become clear. Remove the onions and garlic and set aside in a bowl.

To the same skillet add the chorizo and cook until the chorizo forms an oil. Add the wine to the chorizo and cook for 1-2 minutes then add the shrimp, water, and sugar. Cook for another 1-2 minutes and then add the juice from half of the lemon, the green onions, and the parsley (be sure to chop the parsley and green onions). If you want more sauce add a bit more wine and/or water but be sure to taste as you go.

Cook for 3-5 minutes more and turn off. Remove the salmon from the oven and pour the shrimp and chorizo sauce over the salmon.

Your sauce should not be too thick (you want the texture of a chunky broth). Return to the over for another 15-20 minutes. Remove the dish from the oven and add additional chopped green onions and the other half of the juice from the lemon. Serve with toasted garlic bread. The bread is excellent for dipping into this rich sauce.

Green Curry and Basil Coconut Ribs

Ingredients:
1-2 slabs of pork baby back ribs
2 12-oz cans coconut milk
1 12-oz can coconut cream
½ a Cup of brown sugar
2 jars of Thai green curry paste
2-3 cloves of chopped/minced garlic
Creole seasoning and garlic powder to taste
1 bunch of fresh basil
1 ½ Cups of water

Method:
Wash and clean ribs with cold water. Add ribs to a deep-dish aluminum or roasting pan. Season both sides of the ribs with Creole seasoning and garlic powder. Let sit for about five minutes. Generously add green curry paste to both sides of the rib. Add water to the bottom of the pan and sprinkle the minced garlic over the ribs. Cover with foil and bake at 350° for one hour.

In a large mixing bowl add one can of coconut milk and one can of coconut cream and whisk with brown sugar (taste for sweetness level and be sure you are happy with the taste). Reserve the second can of coconut milk in case you need more sauce for your ribs. Remove ribs from the oven and uncover. If there is still water in the pan drain the majority of the water leaving only a minimal amount at the bottom of the pan. Pour the coconut milk and brown sugar mixture evenly over the ribs. You may need to baste the ribs a bit and move the green curry across the ribs with a spoon to be sure they are evenly coated. Return ribs to oven uncovered and cook on 350° for an additional 30-35 minutes. Check the ribs to make sure they are not browning too quickly. Turn the oven up to 400 for 20-30 minutes checking ribs often to make sure they are becoming caramelized. Once the ribs are golden in color and cooked to your taste remove them from the oven. Let ribs cool for 15-20 minutes or until cool enough to slice. Slice your ribs and garnish with chopped basil. Sometimes I add some basil to the pan while the ribs are still cooking and will pour the excess sauce over the ribs once they are sliced.

Camarones a la Diabla

Ingredients:
2LBS of Shrimp with shell on
3-4 Cans Chipotle peppers in adobo sauce
1 stick of butter
1 bunch of fresh cilantro
3-4 gloves of chopped and minced garlic
3-5 LBS Container of sour cream

Method:
In a large and deep pot melt the butter and add the shrimp. Add garlic to the pot. Let the shrimp and garlic marinate slightly. In a blender mix the chipotle peppers with the sour cream (add as much as you can fit without spilling). Blend until you get a nice creamy mixture. You can add a little water if it's too spicy or too thick. If you want it hotter or less spicy add more peppers or more cream. Once thoroughly blended and spiced to your liking add the sauce to the pot and simmer after mixing well with the shrimp on a low fire for 20-30 minutes. You want to see the oils from the peppers change to an orange-reddish color as you cook the camarones.

Once you are satisfied with the taste of the sauce you can turn off the pot and add as much diced cilantro as you would like both for taste and garnish. I usually mixed some cilantro in and then chop an additional amount on top for garnish.

Couple of tips of adding on to this recipe: You can add chopped chicken breast or thigh meat pieces with the shrimp for something extra special and you can also use any leftover sauce after the shrimp are gone on almost anything: eggs for breakfast, over roasted potatoes, on tacos etc. This is what we call lagniappe (a little something extra) in Louisiana Creole cooking.

Smothered Okra with Chicken, Sausage and Shrimp

Ingredients:
4-6 LBS of chopped fresh or frozen okra.
4-6 large red tomatoes chopped
1lb chicken drumettes
1-2LBS of chopped smoked sausage or andouille chopped
1-2LBS of peeled and deveined shrimp
1 large white or yellow onion chopped and diced
Creole Seasoning
Garlic Powder
4 tablespoons of butter
¼ Cup of vegetable oil
2-3 tablespoons of tomato paste (optional)

Method:
Boil Sausage and slice into small round pieces. Season and lightly fry chicken until brown. In a large pan or skillet (if you have an old electric style skillet for frying chicken this might work best (—the size and depth would be something like a full-sized aluminum pan—). Add the oil to the pan, (you can also use a roasting pan), heat up the oil and add your chopped okra slowly but constantly stirring the okra until it starts to cook down and makes a bit of water and juice. For those who say okra is slimy this is how you "get the slime out." As your okra starts to break down a bit and changes color add your chopped tomatoes to the pan and keep cooking until a juice starts to form. Be sure to add some Creole seasoning and garlic powder. While this is cooking down in a large stock pot add about 1 to 2 cups of water, Creole seasoning, and garlic powder to taste, chopped and diced onion, and half a pound of the smoked sausage and half of the browned chicken. I usually boil and chop the sausage first, so it reduces the amount of oil in the okra. Bring to a boil and add the butter.

Once the butter is melted reduce the fire to low. If you are happy with the texture and sauce that your okra has made you may now add about half of the okra tomato mixture to the pot. Mix thoroughly and add half of the remaining sausage and half of the shrimp. Mix well and taste for seasoning. Now add the remaining okra, sausage, chicken, and shrimp. Let this cook down until you have a rich and reddish juice, seasoning as you go along to your own preferred taste. If you would like a bit more of a red color and tomato taste add the optional tomato paste. Serve over white rice. Some people who like spicy food might add cayenne or Louisiana hot sauce to the pot or to their individual serving. You pick your favorite! In my family we often ate smothered okra with a side of potato salad, fried chicken (yes fried chicken in addition to the one that goes in the okra lol) and maybe sliced cantaloupe. It's a great combination! Give it a try and enjoy.

Caribbean Basa with Coconut Mint and Orange Cream Sauce

Ingredients:
4 Pieces of Basa, Catfish or your favorite fish (the firmer the better)
2 12 oz cans of Coconut Milk
1 12 oz can Coconut Cream
1-2 large oranges
1 bunch of fresh mint
1 bunch of green onions
1/3 Cup brown sugar (or to taste)
Creole seasoning
Garlic Powder

Method:
In a butter greased 13x9 baking dish add your Basa and season on both sides with Creole seasoning and garlic powder. Add your dish to the oven on 350° for about 15-20 minutes. As your fish cooks in a bowl mix the coconut milk, coconut cream, and brown sugar until it meets your taste preference. Remove the fish and add just enough of the coconut cream sauce to cover and coat the fish. Return to the oven for an additional 10 minutes. Slice your oranges into thin round slices and as thick as you would like. Chop up the fresh mint. Remove fish and add the sliced oranges to the sauce being sure

there is enough sauce to cover the oranges and the mint. Let cook for 10-12 minutes and remove from heat. Be sure you have achieved the taste you desire with the mint and orange. The longer you cook the orange and mint the more those flavors will come out.

Serve by itself or over a bed of garlic mashed potatoes or white rice with a side of asparagus and/or a fresh salad. Pairs nicely with white wine.

II. Hatoflvha: Lunch in Louisiana

Black Futurity, Black Joy

"I sing the body electric/ The armies of those I love…/ They will not let me off till I go with them…/ And discorrupt them, and charge them full with the charge of the soul." ~Walt Whitman ("I Sing the Body Electric")

I.
No more crying in pain
No more dying in vain
Ghosts sing a Hallelujah chorus

On broken ankles
angels sprinkle raindrops of freedom
Ancestors rise from fields
rise from ships and seas

No more crying in pain
No more dying in vain
Abolition quest still endless

Black death still fills capitalist cups
Black futures once obscured and unseen in cotton
Black futures once camouflaged by bars and orange jumpsuits
Black futures left fallow on grass fields where cleats till split blood

Not one more *Django*, nor Antebellum,
nor *Get Out* Not even *Roots*
We stand We fight We create circuits
Pools of imagination, designed by grace
Multiple pathways together in song and in light
We become

II.
Remember:
We are JOY
We are JOY
We are JOY

We become connectors, re-building,
re-stitching every fabric. Re-building every Tulsa,
every Congo Square, imagining that New Harlem,
that Oak Town magic, that Caribe beat in Brazil and NOLA

Mardi Gras, Carnival
Life is living

We are conduits faster than
the speed of our own sound
Jazz…Coltrane…Davis
Blues….BB…Holiday….
We ain't no strange fruit
We are First Fruit
We are infinite beginning

Black Circuits to Kinship
Black Circuits to Water Ways
Black Circuits to Ancestors

Our Future is in one another
Our Future is in the circuitry
Our Future is in the ceremony

III.
In the wiping of whip-stained
cracks on our backs
In the wiping of the branded
initials etched in our flesh
we become radioactive resistance through
radical love, for one another
We radiate a circle of love in our songs
We Sing:
I am Black Joy
I am a circuit
I am your medicine

You are Black joy
You are a circuit
You are medicine
We are THE medicine

Hands, hearts, songs connecting
each of our circuits becoming an energy producing
light for our futures we buzz, we dance
we sing a BLACK "body electric"

for our joy...

Black futures
                                    are Black Joy
Black Circuits
                                    are the Routes...

Follow veins the vines of ancestors
Pulsing under skin to
the Routes to Liberation
the Routes to Exhalation

IV.
To sing we must breathe
Breathe in my relative
Breathe in All My Relations
Sing a song again,
Dance a dance again
Pulse through generational electric circuitries

Black Freedom —
I see You

Black Circuitry —
I see you

Black Futurity
I see you...Remember and Sing:
I am Black Joy!
You are Black Joy!
We are Black Joy!

We are electric and infinite

COVID-19 AKA Coronoavirus
"Not wearing a mask/ Is the same as putting your knee/ On my neck..."
~M. Carmen Lane ("Some notes on Racism during a Pandemic")

I.
Infection.
        No cure.
                Weaponized. Pandemic.

But what about
        Running Face Sickness.
                Smallpox.

Where were the masks?
hidden inside diseased blankets
laid upon dead bodies.

        Don't touch me.
        Don't touch that.
        You'll get it.
        They spread it.

"Why do they let them in?"
said my uber driver.
as fear abounds
on planes, in schools, in hospitals,
 places we should feel safe.

Can you hear broken bones crying?

Can you smell ancestors' rotting flesh?
        Now turned to ash...
        Long since decimated...

When we wake—
What fears do we make?
What refusals do we give?
Do we even have a say?

II.
Infection.

        No cure.
                    Weaponized. Pandemic.

Where is humanity in morning light
for blood spilled in dirt and field.
Have they forgotten the dead wombs?
Forgotten diseases still thriving in our colored flesh.

You forget
       we are still here and…
                    Okataktak **isht ikhana yvt falaya.**

III.
Infection.
      No cure.
                Weaponized. Pandemic.
Anti-Black
Mask Off

But who wears which mask?
The smile or the cloth?
Who is smiling?
    Not Black Boys
    Not Black trans women
    Not Breonna
    Not Ahmaud
    Not Harlem
    Not Hunter's Point
    Nor 9th Ward

No — We keep our heads uncovered
for fear on streets, hoodies down
N95 in place we dance bamboula on
busy streets to sidestep

settlers who mask in smiles
telling us… everything is safe.

IV.
Infection.
      No cure.
                Weaponized. Pandemic.

But what about Henrietta Lacks?
What about Tuskegee?
But what about Our Grandmothers?

Where were the masks?
Hidden inside diseased slave ships
nestled into dead bodies.

>	*Don't touch me.*
>	*Don't touch that.*
>	*You'll get it.*
>	*They spread it.*

"Why do they let them in?"
said my uber driver.
Just let us go back to work…
(but where was the work before)
White men in guns and sheets 1850
(Where was the freedom before)
2020 New guns, new sheets, new slaveries
Old pandemics. New names

as fear abounds
on planes, in schools, in hospitals,
places we should feel safe.

Can you hear broken bones crying?

Can you smell ancestors' rotting flesh?
>	Now turned to ash…
>	Long since decimated…

When we wake
What fears do we make?
What refusals do we give?
Do we even have a say?

Forget asking. We shall overcome.
>	We are no longer afraid…

COVID Response

We are not your DISEASE

We thrive.
We will not be your pandemic.
    Your plague.
    Your fear.
    Your climate disaster.
    Your slave.
We refuse.

We refuse to Re/Fuse. So, go on
    Whip your own ass.
    Break your own soul.
    Steal your own land.
    Disease your own children.
Re/Fuse ancestral remedies.

And let us take our hands
stretch them across winds
rivers, and lands unseen.
Grab each other's hands.

Tightly squeezing out in drops
of sweat tinged with blood memory
    Every germ.
    Every lie.
    Every disease.
    Every fear.
We refuse.

That we shall not exist.
That our ancestors did not exist
That our children will not exist
That we shall not remain.

Gran Maître has not called us home yet.

Let us thrive
    Respira

Let us thrive
    Respira
Let us thrive
    Respira
Let us thrive
    Respira

Still…some of use can't breathe.
So, we refuse to Re/Fuse.
    The Heron's memory is long.
Re/Fuse ancestral remedies.
      Let us thrive
      Respira

Gran Maître has not called us home yet.

Rez-Erect Me

Erect this body once more
Erect this spirit in face of your disasters
Speak blasphemies to me like you always do
Wet my member with your adjectives and verbs

Wake me.
Erect me.
Rez-Erect me
if you can.

Each time I open my vessels
your coarse, selfish barbs
rips tendons from flesh

Leaving nothing but more cancerous growth,
tumors engulfing cells of dignity
perverting acts of performance
between our dry sinless sheets

Your teardrops burn holes in sunlit flesh

Wake me.
Erect me.
Rez-Erect me
if you can.

Your pale skin
Your weak emotional capacity
Your sheep in wolves clothing
Those dirty knees lost smells of innocence generations ago

You wreak of privilege
even when you bow down
Mouth Wide Open…
Begging for red cocks to begin new days

        So you can cocka-doodle-doo and
        cocka-doodle-doo over and over again

Your moan more of a whimper
as you scream out:
   Wait. Wait. Wait.
   What do you want from me?
I have given unto you all that god has given to me—
I have nailed my sacredness into your crux-roads

Now together in beds of coal you
push me into death together in beds of
Salvation we do the impossible
We make a crucifixion of love

Wake me.
Erect me.
Rez-Erect me
if you can.

YOU, who never wait
YOU who always ask of others—

Your hand always first,
Your hand always leaving last

Here me
Listen to us
YOU—

The latest in a long line of whoring subversives
drinking blood from bodies of our Christ,
sipping from temples of our flesh.

Erected stone sewn into meat
to be eaten by pale ghosts
You who weaken
dishonoring all that we give

You speak in twisted tongues naming sin
You Blame Them:
                    I Hold You Accountable.
You Burn me over and over again:
                    I Hold You Accountable.

You stick me on that Rez-ervation List:
                         I Hold You Accountable.

Cold feet don't allow oxygen to circulate —
Turn blue, mouth won't open and
Your breath won't cum —
Because you are entangled in your own
                         Bullshit!

Bullshit stretched on long roads
Where you learned from master's house of tools
Bult yourself another trophy,
So you can shine, —
                         Not us.
 So YOU are fed —
                         not US.

Here me.
Listen to us.
YOU —

I'm done with forgiving
                         We're done with forgetting
I've done all I can to trust, to give,
to sacrifice, to heal, to love
                         We are done.

I refuse to lose yet again
another part of myself
to your madness and fear

Wake me.
Erect me.
Rez-Erect me
if you can.

Was it August or October?
~For the one who loves "flats" only

Was it August or October?
I know it was on Grindr.
Maybe I never told you.
Your eyes, I wondered
"Are they real?"

The color was an
Intoxicating poison,
or maybe like Wonder Woman
they lassoed me.

Caught.
You roped me in.
Maybe you didn't want to,
maybe I wanted you to…
Hell, who Knows

I cannot only taste, but I can smell that kiss. Do you remember? The one in the car? In the hills? Your brother's car. We met at the lake Did you know that lake is the oldest? The oldest wildlife refuge in the United States. That's right 1870. I probably told you this before. You know I repeat myself. I'm getting older…

My mother always said I had a memory like her. Really, I got my heart from her. And maybe, just maybe, that's why we met in that place. A place of refuge. It was safe. Sheltered.

Not like my body.
Filled with stories.
Filled with rivets from needles.
Leftovers from incessant
blood draws, to this
body, pulled down
to underworlds weights
pulling balls of my feet. Down
through the bottom of earth's center.
Can you feel the water
rushing into my flesh?

Was it August or October? I know it was 2013. We kept coming back... But never to the refuge. Never to the Lake. We were right there. Close. Close to where the street bends. Where the bakery once stood. It was Baggy's...What a first date.

We ate a lot. We tasted a lot. We had this rhythm, this synching. But then I rose, and you remained. All day. You remained...

Remained in the sheets.
In the sweat of our pasts.
In the silence of our aftermath.
Traumas colliding.
You told me.
I didn't listen.

Birds of paradise were the first and last flowers. Whitney was playing on repeat, of course. Did you know that Whitney means, "white water?" It is a town in England. We never got to go. We never got to ride on the water.

Was it August or October?
The month, the day...
It doesn't matter.
It was real.
Our refuge.
It broke.

All the cracks in an earth that devastates children. That steals youth. That silences love and possibility. This place could not be our forever refuge. So, we walk to the water once more...

We both love water.
But I can't swim.
You are a fish.
You just keep diving and going.
Diving and going...

Alone.

I'm right here standing in the light

Feet to sand
Feet to sand
Feet to sand...

Stable.
I remember you.
I remember you,
from the place of unknowing.

Men can't go there "Too Soft," or "Too Weak." Softness and vulnerability it sinks. Sinks dreams. Sinks love. Sinks bravery. You were brave once. I was too.

We didn't make it easy. We didn't let ourselves go to that place, to sanctuary. It is in the refuge of where we first and last met. Between the waters of the Bay and Coronado. It's behind the place in our eyes where only we can see.

It wasn't March...nor February when we said goodbye. For love comes rushing away just as quickly as the wave on which she came rushing to shore. It wasn't August or October.

But it was a moment.
Just moment
OF FOREVER

Hyphy

"That a war of extermination will continue to be waged between the races until the Indian race becomes extinct must be expected. While we cannot anticipate this result but with painful regret, the inevitable destiny of the race is beyond the power or wisdom of man to avert."~ Peter Burnett, first Governor of California[6]

Born at intersection of the same black-brown streets.
Flooded by the same poverty-stricken bullets.
"I come from East Oakland where the youngstas get hyphy"[7]

>You eat
>>while we starve.
>
>You eat and forget
>>what hunger feels like.
>
>Cuz after all if we be hungry
>>"let them eat grass or their own dung."[8]

Cuz you just don't care to remember —
Remember and recognize
your own hurt,
your own anger,
your own suffering.

Here we stand — you against us.
On what side of history shall you reside?
Are you a marble statue like Columbus?
Will you couch our hunger in paternal patriarchy?
Our founding fathers?
Or like those before you continue to forget us?

Will it be at the boot of your own creation?
Will it be at the boot of a colonial master you refuse not to serve?
Will you cut off your heart to spite your pride?
Will you wear their mask?

While you eat at the master's table,
gaining more coin year after year —

---

[6] "State of the State Address," January 6, 1851
[7] Too$hort, "Blow the Whistle," from the album of the same name.
[8] Andrew Jackson Myrick, settler representative for traders in Dakota territories, 1862.

your salary rises — 300 thousand, 400 thousand —
Going going going — GONE!
It's out of here!

You have hit a home run with your salary, Mr. President!
While colored bodies are pushed out, shot up,
dis(membered), written out of even your own existence —

>   You eat
>   while we starve.
>   You eat and forget
>   what hunger feels like.
>   Kill our kin and wait, cuz
>   "Every buffalo dead is an Indian gone
>   literally overnight."[9]

Here you eat and we starve —
As you build up your sports teams,
watching all the games.
Yet students starve while your
Ego is all you can bare to save.

 You may come from East Oakland, but you ain't never been hyphy.

You ain't been hyphy cuz you can't remember
or see ancient streets where Black, Red, and Brown
mothers toiled on broken backs, while melanated fathers
had their pride beaten out in repetitions
until they got no more breath to breathe —
But yeah, you made it.
Got your piece of the pie.

What ceremony will you create with it?
What meals will you cook?
How you gonna nourish souls of a thousand ancestors?

What Spirit?
What Student?

---

[9] U.S. Army Colonel, Richard Irving Dodge.

Who can you love with
the love of your grandparents,
your aunties, your ancient ones—
when you play wypipo politics?

>You eat
>>while we starve.
>You eat and forget
>>what hunger feels like.
>Cuz after all if we be hungry
>>"let them eat grass or their own dung."

You eat, while we starve on broken budgets.
Choking on every broken promise.

You all the broken treaties,
You all the stolen legacies,
You put you and you and you

Before WE.
Before US.
Before Humanity.

No room for us at your inn.
So, you starve your faculty.
Starve your staff.
You starve our students,
our community.
You starve all who await your word.
All who await to find your honor.

>You eat
>>while we starve.
>You eat and forget
>>what hunger feels like.
>Kill our kin and wait, cuz
>>"Every buffalo dead is an Indian gone
>literally overnight."

You eat at tables of false idols,
false truths, unlearned histories—

twisted for your own version of reality.

Are you on east 14th or International?
Whose histories do you remember?
You caught that historical amnesia?
Cuz, you ain't remembering our history together.

You may come from East Oakland, but ya ain't hyphy.

You eat and we starve.
In the end you gonna with us.
Cuz no unremembering severs pain
deeply buried in your own heart.

> "Let them eat grass or their own dung."
> "Every buffalo dead is an Indian gone literally overnight."

Close your eyes.
Can you hear Too$hort?
Do you know or remember who he is?

Fall from hyphy to "civilized."
Fall from ceremonial and communal
to individual got you seeking to
institutionalize ethnic studies
Killing transforms to higher education
where we lay slaughtered in fields of academic disciplines.

What does your meal really cost?

Don't ya see?
We can all eat.
When we let the SYSTEM starve.

RECIPES

Andrew's Opelousas-Cali Sausage, Chicken and Shrimp Jambalaya Topped with Fried Catfish and Crab Legs

Ingredients:
4-6 Cups Rice cooked
2 Green Bell Peppers chopped
2-3 Yellow or White Onions chopped
1 Cup of Vegetable oil
1 8 oz can of Tomato Sauce (you may want a second can just in case)
1 6 oz can of Tomato Paste
1 Cup of Green Onions
1 Cup of fresh Parsley
1 additional bunch of fresh Parsley for garnish
4 lemons
3-4 Cloves of chopped and minced Garlic
Creole Seasoning
Garlic Powder
1 LB Smoked Sausage or Andouille
1 LB Shrimp peeled and deveined
1 LB of Chopped Chicken breast or thigh meat
1-2 Cups of water or chicken broth
4 pieces of boneless, skinless catfish
3-4 clusters of snow crab or blue crab

1 stick of butter

Method:
In a large (ideally cast iron) skillet mix the heated vegetable oil with the bell pepper, onions (white and green), garlic and parsley. Cook until the vegetables are tender. Add Creole seasoning and Garlic powder to taste. Add tomato sauce and paste and blend well.

Reduce and cook on low for 30-45 minutes stirring occasionally then remove from heat. Boil your sausage and chicken and cool before slicing into bit sized pieces. Cook 4-6 cups of white rice. In a large and deep-dish 2" full sized aluminum pan add enough butter to grease the entire pan. In a large stock pot add the cooked rice, chicken broth or water along with your tomato sauce mixture, the chopped chicken and sausage and the uncooked shrimp. Add seasoning to taste and mix well.

Add the jambalaya to the buttered aluminum pan adding a bit of sliced butter (about 4-6 thin slices) to the top and about half a cup of additional broth or water (you don't have to add the additional water/broth but if you want a more tender or saucy jambalaya this should do it). Cover with foil and cook in the oven on 350° for 30-45 minutes.

While the jambalaya cooks, season and batter your fish (slice the four pieces in half so that you have 8 total pieces) in flour and fry all 8 pieces for about 8-10 minutes or until golden brown. Remove from heat. Boil your crabs in 2-3 cups of water with 1 stick of butter, Creole seasoning, and garlic powder with about two teaspoons of lemon juice. Remove crab from juice and separate the clusters once cooled. Uncover the jambalaya and stir. Be sure everything is thoroughly mixed and that you are happy with the flavor and seasoning level. You can add additional tomato sauce it you feel it needs it but be sure to add more seasoning to balance the taste. Return to oven on 400 for about 15-20 minutes and remove from heat.

Place the fried catfish on top of the jambalaya in the center and add the crab legs around the outside area of the pan. Add sliced lemon wedges and fresh parsley to the corners and middle of the pan for final presentation.

Shrimp, Crab, and Crawfish Étouffée

Ingredients:
1 LB Shrimp
1 LB Crab
1-2 LBS Crawfish
1 Green Bell Pepper
1 Red Bell Pepper
2-3 Stalks of Celery
1 Yellow or White Onion
1 Bunch of Fresh Parsley
2 Cups of White Flour
4 Sticks of Butter
32 oz of Chicken or Seafood Stock
Creole Seasoning
Garlic Powder

Method:
In a stockpot melt the butter. Once melted and hot slowly add the flour starting with one cup. The more flour you add the thicker the "gravy" of your étouffée will be. Add at least half of the second cup of flour then add Creole seasoning and garlic powder and whisk rapidly until the mixture gets to a dark brown color and is fairly thick, you may decide to add the remaining flour. Once you achieve a nice brown color add your chopped and diced vegetables except for the parsley. Then add half of the chicken or seafood stock and stir until the mixture becomes somewhat thin. Be sure to reduce the heat once you add the broth and vegetables. Add a bit more seasoning in the remaining broth.

Let this simmer for about 20-25 minutes. In the meantime, make sure you peel and clean all of your shrimp. For the crab you will want to use a can or container of crab claw meat, unless you have fresh claws. Add your seafood to the étouffée and stir thoroughly adding any additional seasoning you may want at this time. Cover and cook on low for about 20-30 minutes. Add half of the bunch of the parsley chopped to the pot for the last 10-15 minutes that your étouffée cooks. Serve over white rice. I enjoy fried chicken with my plate of étouffée and/or a side of potato salad!

Garlic & Butter Roasted Chicken Stuffed with a Shrimp, Crab and Bacon Dressing

Ingredients:
1 3-4 LB Chicken
1-2 Sticks of Butter
1 LB of Peeled Shrimp
1 12-16 oz Can of Crab Claw Meat
6 Slices of Bacon
2 Boxes of Jiffy Corn Bread Mix
12-24 oz of Chicken Broth
3 Cups of Milk
2 Eggs
2-3 Tablespoons of Vegetable Oil
1 Large White or Yellow Onion
1 Bunch of Green Onions
1 Red Bell Pepper
1 Green Bell Pepper
Creole Seasoning
Garlic Powder

Method:
In a large bowl mix together two boxes of jiffy cornbread mix, 2 eggs, and 2 cups of milk. I make the batter for jiffy much thinner than most people and admittedly I don't measure how much milk, so this is an estimate as is the case with most of these recipes. You want a thin almost pancake-like batter (perhaps thinner) texture. You may add a 3rd cup milk to achieve this consistency. In a large oven safe (preferably cast iron) skillet add about 2-3 tablespoons of vegetable oil and place in a pre-heated oven on 400° for about 5 mins. Remove skillet from oven and add the cornbread mixture. Cook until golden brown (about 20-25 minutes). Add a few slices of butter to the top for the last 5-7 minutes.

While your cornbread cooks melt half a stick of butter in a large and deep skillet. To the melted butter add the chopped onions (white and green), bell peppers, and if you'd like you can also add two cloves of chopped garlic. Cook the vegetables on low until they become somewhat soft (about 10-12 minutes). Set vegetables to the side and fry your bacon and set to the side. Now once you have removed your cornbread from the oven set this to the side and let it cool for about 15 minutes. Wash and clean your chicken and season on the inside and outside with Creole seasoning and garlic powder. Place the chicken in a large roasting pan and add a tiny bit of water to the bottom of the pan about half a cup. Now in large stock pot or pan mix your cornbread and vegetables and chicken stock, crab, bacon, and shrimp, additional seasoning and about a half a stick of butter until you achieve the texture and taste you desire. Be sure to mix and cook thoroughly for about 10 minutes.

Let the seafood dressing cool and stuff as much as you want into your chicken (careful not to over stuff or your chicken won't cook through). I usually stuff the chicken and then add the extra dressing to the sides of the same pan where the chicken is cooking, or it may be cooked in a separate pan on 350° for about 35-45 minutes. Your chicken stuffed with dressing will cook on 350° for at about two hours. You will want to add slices of butter to your chicken and turn up the temperature to 400° for the last 10 minutes of cook time.

Ribeye Steak and Mango Salsa Frybread Sliders

Ingredients:
3-4 Cups of Self-Rising Flour
1-2 Cups of Water
2-3 Ribeye Steaks
Creole Seasoning
Garlic Powder
2 Ripe Mangos
2 Red Tomatoes
2-3 Jalapeno or Habanero Peppers
1 White or Yellow Onion
3 Cloves of Mince Garlic
1/3 Cup of Minced or Diced Cilantro
2 Cups of Vegetable Oil

Method:
In a large mixing bowl add 3-4 cups of self-rising flour, 1 cup of water and blend well. If it is too dry add the second cup of water. Mix well (use your hands or a spoon), adding more flour or water as needed to get a soft but non-sticky dough. Form dough into round balls and let sit for a few minutes. You should be able to make about 8-10 pieces of frybread depending on size of each piece. In a deep skillet heat 1 ½ to 2 cups of vegetable oil. Once your oil his hot take your balls of dough and flatten each piece poking a small hole in the center of each piece and fry them one or two at a time depending on the size of the skilled for 3-4 minutes. Generally, unless you have a deep fryer, you will want to fry one piece at a time. Brown on each side. Once all the frybread is done remove and layout on napkins or paper bags to absorb the oil.

Meanwhile season your ribeye steaks with Creole seasoning, garlic powder, and either fry for about 8 minutes (4 one side and 3-4 on the other) or grill your steaks. Once steaks are done chop each streak into bite sizes pieces. Now in a medium bowl add chopped mango, half of the chopped onion, the cilantro, chopped garlic, tomatoes, peppers and mix well. You may add a pinch or two of salt if you'd like and if you want a slightly more citrus flavor you can add 1-2 teaspoons of lime juice. Mix well. Add the chopped ribeye meat to your individual pieces of frybread and top with your mango salsa. Goes great with a glass of sangria or lemonade.

Pork Belly Mac and Cheese

Ingredients:
3LBS of medium elbow macaroni noodles
¼ Cup Vegetable Oil
2 LBS Sharp Cheddar Cheese
1 lb Mild Cheddar Cheese
2 LBS Monterrey Jack Cheese
1-2 LBS of Pork Belly
2 Cups of Water
4-6 Cups of Milk
2 Sticks of Butter
Salt
Black Pepper
Seasoning Salt or Creole Seasoning
5-6 Eggs
2LB bag of shredded cheese blend

Method:
Season your pork belly with Creole seasoning and garlic powder and let sit for 15-20 minutes. In a medium skillet add about 3-4 tablespoons of vegetable oil. Once the oil is hot add your pork belly braising the meat on each side for about 3 minutes per side or until golden and crisp. Remove your pork belly and add it to a large baking pan with about 1-2 cups of water. Add additional seasoning to the water and any of the juices from the skillet you used to fry the meat. Cover with foil and bake on 350° for about 2 hours or until the meat is very tender. For the last 15 minutes uncover and turn heat up to 400° to get the pork belly crispy.

Meanwhile fill a large stock pot with water about 3/4th full. Bring to a boil adding 2-3 teaspoons of salt and vegetable oil. Once its boiling add your macaroni stirring occasionally until the noodles are fully cooked (about 15-25 minutes). Once your noodles are fully cooked strain them noodles and cool with cold water. Then add noodles to a deep-dish aluminum baking pan. Add salt and pepper to the noodles. Shred your pork belly and add it to the noodles stirring well. Add as much of the cheddar and Monterey cheese as you would like. Mix in sliced pieces of 1 stick of butter and blend well.

In a large bowl mix the milk, eggs, pepper, and seasoning salt until the eggs are fully blended. Pour this mixture over the macaroni. If you need additional milk/eggs feel free to add more but this should be sufficient. You can shake a little pepper over the macaroni and if you need additional cheese use the shredded blend. Place in the oven covered with foil and bake on 350° for about 1 hour or until fully cooked and golden brown on top. You may remove the foil for the last 15-20 minutes and add additional butter to give the top a nice golden crust.

Roasted Pork Tenderloin in a Blackberry Pear Sauce over Spinach, Blue Cheese, and Bacon Salad

Ingredients:
2 pork tenderloin
Creole Seasoning
Garlic Powder
4 Chopped Garlic Cloves
2 Bunches of Spinach
6 Slices of Bacon
1 LB Crumbled Blue Cheese
5 18 oz containers of fresh blackberries
6-8 Green Pears Chopped and peeled
2-3 Cups of white sugar
6 Cups of Water
2 Tablespoons Cinnamon
1 tablespoon Nutmeg
2 Tablespoons Vanilla
1/2 Stick of Butter

Method:
Begin by adding 2 tablespoons of olive oil to a large skillet. Then

season each pork tenderloin with Creole seasoning and garlic powder. Using a thin knife insert holes on both sides of the roast and stuff the holes with the chopped garlic. Turn your skillet to high and once the oil is hot add one tenderloin to the skilled and lightly brown on both sides. Remove the first tenderloin and add the second repeating the browning method (about 3-5 minutes total). To a large roasting pan add 2 cups of water. Add seasoning to the water and then add the pork tenderloins covering with foil. Place in the oven and bake at 350 for an hour and a half.

While your tenderloins bake peel and dice your pears. In a large stock pot add 3-4 cups of water, the diced pears and blackberries, sugar, cinnamon, nutmeg, vanilla, and butter bringing to a boil. You want to cook this on a high heat for about an hour or until the fruit breaks down and begins to caramelize and becomes thick. You may have to add more sugar in order to do this. You can taste and add additional spices or sugar as you go to achieve the taste and texture of a semi thick sauce. Once your sauce is done remove from heat and set to the side.

Fry your bacon and pat dry with paper towels to remove excess grease. Remove the foil from your tenderloins and turn up the heat to 400° and cook for an additional 20-30 minutes until fully cooked, tender, and golden brown. Once your tenderloin is done remove from the oven and set aside. In a large skillet melt 2 tablespoons of butter and add your spinach and sauté until your spinach is tender (about 3-5 mins). Remove spinach from heat and let it rest. In a large 13 x 9 serving dish add all your spinach so the dish is evenly spread across. Now using kitchen scissors add chopped pieces of bacon evenly across the spinach. Finish by adding as much crumbled blue cheese across the dish as you would like. Lastly, top the spinach, bacon and blue cheese with both tenderloins setting them at an angle and unsliced. Drizzle your blackberry pear sauce across each tenderloin reserving the remainder for individual servings.
This is presentation ready, and you will want to slice the tenderloin which should be very tender and serve each plate with a bit of the spinach, bacon, and blue cheese mixture with extra blackberry pear sauce in a serving bowl for those who would like it. I often have extra sauce and can them and serve for other things like pancakes, French toast, or anything you would like to add an extra special taste to.

III. Pimen Dou: Dinner and Dancin

Give it All to the People
"You know we've got to find a way/ To bring some lovin' here today"~ Marvin Gaye, ("What's Going On")

When shadows come
When disaster strikes
When sorrows invade
    Give it All to the People

Give your love
Give your heart
Give your commitment
    Give it All to the People

When you fear failure,
When you're silenced by machines,
and you have lost your will
When you lose sight of footprints in sand
    Give it All to the People

Give your breath
Give your light,
Give your vulnerability
    Give it All to the People

Make the People your Sacred Love
Find salvation in the shifting sands of immortality
Make love to justice
Make love across city streets

When all around you seems unforgiving

Give breath
Give spirit
Give talent
Give your will
    Give it All to the People

Give as it has been given to you

The People

Mothers, Grandmothers
The People
Fathers, Grandfathers
The People
Ancestors, Ancient Ones
    Give it as it has been Given to You

Let us whisper beauty through concrete walls
Whisper beauty through institutional systems
Whisper beauty in day and in night

    Give it All to the People

Remember —
Give and become free
Give and become flesh
We are of and by the People
Flesh of the all the People.

Let light bring re-birth
Let spirit link you
to all the Ancient Ones

Become the Answer
Become ALL of the People

You are sacred
We are sacred
You are sacred
We are and always
SACRED

In God's Own Image

In God's Own Image we are made and re-made.
In imperfection
       in silence,
              in fear —
                      and against all that is taboo.
In God's Own Image light remains our guide,
and truth becomes our constant.

No one lives without fear,
       without secrets,
              without desires.
No one seeks the harder road.
       No one chooses the disavowed and socially hated.

              Man makes distance.
              Man builds walls.
              Man destroys our freedom
              to be present in our own truth,
              in our own light
              in our own grace.

Let today be our awakening to new journeys,
to new pathways —
       To open hearts, arms, and minds.
Let our wings be set free to find morning air
       rising once more.
Let sunsets be our prayer of return.
Let kindness and new experiences be our riverbank retreat.

              Let our images,
              Let our truths,
              Let our bodies —

Open so we can genuflect
upon soft pillows of our own choosing.
So, we can be at peace in dark as in light —
Without fear, without judgement, without disgrace.

For we are God's Own Image

We are God's Dreams
Creations in love come to life.

Where dreams of all manifestations and pairings of love can stand
where bodies can intertwine and dance and love and just be.
We are the love born from God's Own Image

So, take breath,
        Take pause—
                Just live this one life

                      This one life.
            Give yourself permission for joy.
              Made in God's Own Image.

Enraptured

Unspeakable presence
Unspeakable joy
Under a quiet evening moon

I began to speak with this old
oak tree my ancient ancestor

You were revealed to me in a dream
A dream I had thought was dying
Enraptured in your smiling kindness
Enraptured in the heat behind your dark eyes

Forecasting not tomorrow — Just Today
Forecasting not futures — Just Present
Forecasting Light and Grace

Not too many seas between
Not too many oceans to cross

For time and distance cannot contain that which
begins as cocoon and emerges from crusting black
sands into multi-colored butterflies of transformation

You unearth every cave in me
You unearth every vulnerability —
waiting to excite to life

We are the Wali Kukula
We are the Junglefowl —
Singing upon uncut colored tongues

When we begin the earth rotates in the distance
enraptured once more by the sighting of our touch
    There is still hope

I'll sip the wine from your lips
I'll be the cloak to cover your crooked unbroken halo

You enrapture my spirit with your hands

Pressed against soft wet skin
You enrapture my soul with your ear
pressed against my rib
You enrapture my heart with your gentle
yet affirming words
You enrapture me with deeds and reminders —

You are my shield
You are my sacred
You are my awakening —

You are my today
My moment
My here — My NOW

I smell still the unknown
scent of your fragrance

I am enraptured
I am enraptured
I am enraptured —

Inside of YOU

I am enraptured
I am enraptured —
    In Us

You Compliment Me
"Look what happens with A love like that, / It lights the Whole Sky." ~Hafiz

Your look is not complete or void
    You compliment me.

I grow again and again at each sighting of your smile
    You compliment me.

Your words deepen each unknown moment
    You compliment me.

Knowing and speaking not cerebrally but bodily,
breathing life into words, your scent like your touch
brings heat, calm, rejuvenation, eradicates complication

In your arms peace envelops me
silencing unexpressed fear, I am
finally unleashed and I believe in our

unknown path, in our untold beginning,
we reconcile our unsettled present, knowledge
held in these bodies together, eradicates complication

I hold your image etched in my skin,
stained in my blood, stitched together by
ancestors of different shores on islands and bayous

In sacred tongues of forgiving grace
    You compliment me.

No distance, no tears, no other yearning
just this now, just us and eyes speaking polyvocal
emotions with ancestral tongues all at once

We are born unto each other again and again
    From water and earth.
We are born from all that is forgiving
    From air and fire.

We are stones of malleable miracles

re-born again unto and into one another
rising like new grass after each spring rain

You and I are not complete,
we are entangled spirits,
we are not chains, nor chained
We are freedom
      You compliment me.

In sun and shade,
with love and hands clasped
together like revolutionary rings.

      You compliment me.

Not One Word

I've written a love poem before.
Many times before.
Tonight, your face appears.

Again.

After centuries of remembering the curves of
untouched skin upon your face
You appear—

Again.

In a flash of many colors
and in many truths—
In a flash of radiant energy

You warm me, remind me how
I might enter again step in pace with
ancient ones, yet with gentleness of a newborn

I search this aging and ageless brain
for one word, but not
ONE word came.

No, it is many words coming
over and over again, rolling in tides
carrying words like songs of your spirit:

> *It's his strength.*
> *It's his truth.*
> *It's his laugh.*
> *It's his unwavering Virgo spirit!*

You change me, move me, intrigue and
inspire. You breathe into me a spirit
I used to know, and today before all the spirits between us—

I reclaim it. We reclaim it.
Upon the backs of a dozen broken winged birds—

seeking their own refuge

This refuge brings answers to age old questions.
Refuge brings truths to the mysteries of love and life.
This refuge brings poems for new lovers.

Your appearance from out of the corner darkness of evening sky
bursts into a billion stars across waters of my soul, where I close
my eyes remembering you from across the seas

Of years already gone by
in past lives, in day and in night—
You appear—

Again.

So, not one word describes what we have grown
Not one word describes what we will become
Not one word explains what we remember

I've written a love poem before.
Many times before.
But with you this poem is re-written—

                        Again and again.

A Thousand Times
~For the One Who Loves Hibiscus

I apologize for a thousand years of wounds unleashed on beds of hidden water, deep beneath what is me. Deep beneath what is humanity.

I apologize for a thousand years of colonization on children's hearts that become adult bodies, with adult selfishness, and individual abandon.

I apologize for a thousand years of bound up and broken hopes for better tomorrows, for better friendships, for stronger community between us.

I apologize on feet of ash and coal
with words muted by untamed pain.

I breathe my love.
I breathe my spirit.
I breathe all that I hold.
I breathe all that I hope to be renewed.
I breathe all of this…

Into You.

JCB
~ pour Justicia, Cariño, y Belleza

I.
Like waves of two oceans meeting
Like solar system awakenings

Bright morning rises
no distance
Strong force
openings at dusk

Meet me here again
in this place

With fortitude
we are guided by
dreams that we become

What ancestors have recorded

Justicia, Cariño, y Belleza

I am for you all that
dust turns to flesh
back to dust again

Ashes turn to seeds
We are planted
in this time of destined caminos,
paths intertwined

II.
This path lit along nuestro malecón
caminando mano en mano
respirando el aire de los santos

You are my warmth.
You are my Venus and
I am unscorched in your radiance

We are planted
in this softening molten rock
buoyant in our return

Firm in this commitment
It is for Justice
It is for Love
It is for Beauty

Justicia, Carino, y Belleza

Initials etched in sand
with memories still becoming
memories growing
momento a momento

III.
There in the shadows
we awaken
new life springs

Hard-work
Familia
Endurance
Cultura
Community

These are vows and values

Together emerging
beneath long since grassed over
forgotten landscapes

We traverse once more

The place where love lights
the sun keeping
a generation whole

Connecting our spirits
once more with the
love of a thousand romances

Love of a thousand movements,
gifted to us in stone
by a thousand ancestors

IV.
This our birth right
Our destiny

Climb the hill
look out and behold
all the universe

For them
For us
For life
For…

Justicia, Carino, y Belleza

Thrivance

"I got swamp water runnin' through my veins /The Mississippi river can't be tamed..."~ The Neville Brothers ("Fire on the Bayou") [10]

The smoke from the boucherie fire still burns
smoked meats and fried gratons fill our stomachs.
There along the water they keep dancing.
There hidden in the bayou
children keep dancing.

> Say, "they out there stomping again!"
> "Ain't nothing wrong with dat, yea!"
> "We gots to keep eating, mais yea!"

My great-grandmother, they called her Nanan,
she was a traituer and a quilt maker.
The patches make a pattern.
Make a circuit.

> Say, "Who ya people be?"
> "You a Guillory?!"
> "What you say cher!"
> "Me Too...I'm kin to the Guillory"

We are patterns sewn
together by old wrinkled hands
and fat swollen thumbs
dangling from Nanan's big arms

Big arms from spinning spoons in the gumbo pot.
Big arms from tapping our behinds with a switch
from the magnolia trees. We still standing here...

But we march too.
We have done more than survive.
Who say we are forgotten?

I remember.

---

[10] written by Leo Nocentelli, Ziggy Modeliste, Art Neville, Cyril Neville, George Porter Jr.

You remember.
WE REMEMBER!

Remember
our birthplace,
our land,
our water
our songs.

So, we sing again.
We stomp our feet on the ground.
Where Nanan stopped bleeding with her medicines.

We stomp our feet where Pop fed the people.
The cotton fills the quilts and the crawfish
still float to the top when we flood them out.

Creation begins with
all our relations.
So, we stomp
and we live.

We begin again
We thrive.
We thrive.
We thrive.

We are circuits
connecting Pasts to Presents,
singing songs for our Futures.
We are a People.

So, let us thrive.
Let us thrive.
We will thrive.

RECIPES

Creole Stuffed Chile Relleno Peppers

Ingredients:
6-8 Chile Relleno Peppers
1LB of Shrimp
5 Strips Bacon fried
1LBS Crab Claw Meat
1 Yellow Onion diced
1 Green Bell Pepper diced
1 Red Bell Pepper diced
3 Cloves of Garlic diced
1 Can of Breadcrumbs or Panko Flakes
Creole Seasoning
Garlic Powder
1-2 Sticks Butter
Parmesan or Cheddar Cheese, freshly grated

Method:
In a large skillet melt the butter (use both sticks if you want a richer sauce but if you're watching your cholesterol you can just use one). To the butter add all the chopped vegetables. Once the vegetables are soft (about 5 minutes) add your shrimp, crab, chopped bacon and breadcrumbs along with the Creole seasoning and garlic powder and blend well cooking for about 10 minutes. Be sure to

add enough breadcrumbs to thicken up your stuffing for the peppers. Let your stuffing cool.

Meanwhile wash and slice your peppers in half removing all the seeds. With a spoon generously stuff each pepper and top with parmesan cheese and bake in the oven on 350° for about 30 minutes or until fully cooked and golden brown on top! These make either nice appetizers for a party or can be served as meal along with a nice side salad and white or red wine!

Baked Cushaw (Squash)

Ingredients:
8-10 Pattypan Squash
2 Cups White Sugar
6 Slices of White Bread
2 Eggs
3 Teaspoons Vanilla Extract
Cinnamon
Nutmeg
1 Stick Butter

Method:
Peel and boil the squash until tender. Remove squash from water and mash with a potato masher or large spoon. Add the strips of bread and mix until smooth and well blended. You may add 1-2 teaspoons of flour for a firmer consistency. Add half a stick of softened butter, cinnamon (about 2-3 tablespoons), nutmeg (about 1 teaspoon), vanilla, sugar, and eggs and blend well. In a 13 x 9 glass casserole dish use the other half stick of butter to grease the pan lightly. Pour the Cushaw batter into the pan spreading evenly then bake in the oven on 350° for about 45-55 minutes or until fully cooked and slightly golden brown on top. This was a dish my grandmother made every Christmas Eve and it holds very special memories for me. May it bring you joy as well!

Crab and Lobster Bisque

Ingredients:
2 Sticks Butter
1 Bunch Green Onions
2-3 Cups of Milk
1 Cup Heavy Whipping Cream
4 Slices Bacon
Creole Seasoning
Garlic Powder
Half of a Yellow or White Onion
1-2 Teaspoons of Worcestershire Sauce
2-3 Lobster Tails
1 16 Can Crab Claw Meat
2 Teaspoons of Tomato Paste
4-5 Tablespoons of Flour
3 Tablespoons of grated Cheddar Cheese
16-32 oz Chicken or Seafood Broth

Method:
Melt butter in a large stock pot. Once melted add the milk and whipping cream, Creole seasoning, and garlic powder to taste. Let simmer for about 10 minutes then add chopped green and white onions, Worcestershire sauce, tomato paste, flour, and cheese. Let this simmer for an additional five minutes then add the chicken broth (use as much as you want to make enough servings for the size of your dinner/event) and let cook for 15-20 minutes adding seasoning to taste. Add the chopped fried bacon to the pot along the crab and the lobster. Be sure to remove the crab from shells and chop into small pieces. Let cook for another 15 minutes and serve with sliced bread.

Crawfish, Sausage, Shrimp, and Crab Fettucine

Ingredients:
3 16oz packages Fettucine Pasta
1LB Smoked Sausage or Andouille
1LB Shrimp
1LB Crab Claw Meat
2 Sticks Butter
1 Red Bell Pepper chopped
1 Yellow or White Onion chopped
1 Green Bell Pepper chopped
1 Bunch Green Onions chopped
2 Celery Stalks chopped
3-4 Cloves Garlic diced
4-5 Tablespoons of Flour
Creole Seasoning
Cayenne Pepper
Garlic Powder
1 Package Velveeta Cheese
1 Cup Parmesan Cheese
¼ Cups Fresh Parsley diced
3 Cups Half and Half or Heavy Whipping Cream
1 32 oz bag Shredded Cheddar Cheese

Method:
This is an intense and rich dish. It is meant to serve a large amount of people and it is a party favorite in Houston and Louisiana. You may substitute and reduce it to a smaller recipe by cutting the ingredients by a third or half depending on how much you want to make. The first step is to prep all your ingredients by chopping all of the vegetables. Boil your sausage first and cut in ¼ inch slices. Next in a very large stock pot boil all your fettucine with a little salt and vegetable oil and stir occasionally to keep the pasta from sticking. Be sure your water is boiling before you place the noodles in the water. Once done, strain the noodles and rinse with cool water. Pour the noodles into a large deep-dish full-sized aluminum pan and season generously with Creole seasoning and garlic powder and as much cayenne seasoning as you would like. You may also add fresh black pepper. Mix well and add your chopped sausage into the pan and mix in well so there is sausage evenly spread throughout the pan of noodles.

Next in a large stock pot melt your butter and add in the half and half/whipping cream and add a bit of Creole seasoning and garlic powder. Next add the Velveeta cheese and cook until it is completely melted. To the sauce add all your chopped vegetables (garlic, bell pepper, onions, celery, green onions) once your vegetables have softened a bit add to the sauce your shrimp (completely peeled and cleaned) and your crab meat and blend well and cook for about 10-15 minutes. If you feel you need more sauce at any time you can add additional half and half, be sure to season to taste as you mix everything.

Once your sauce is done pour it over your pan of noodles and sausage and mix very thoroughly until everything is evenly spread out add seasoning as you mix the pasta and at this stage you can sprinkle in a little of the shredded cheddar cheese to ensure you have a cheesy enough pasta. Once satisfied smooth out the top of the pasta and sprinkle the top with just a little of the cheddar cheese then cover with foil and bake on 350° for about an hour or an hour and a half. After cooking for about 45 mins remove the foil so that your top can crust and brown. Remove and serve. This pasta goes great alone or as a side for a family BBQ.

Andrew's Shrimp & Beef Burgers

Ingredients:
1LB Ground Beef, Turkey, or Pork
1LB Chopped Shrimp
1 Bunch Green Onions
1 Bunch Fresh Parsley
3-4 Cloves Garlic chopped
Creole Seasoning
Garlic Powder
Smoked Paprika

Method:
In a mixing bowl add your ground meat of choice along with the chopped shrimp (after peeling and cleaning the shrimp cut them in half or into three pieces so they are bite sized), seasonings, and all vegetables and blend well. Form each burger into patties of your choice and fry them for about 8-10 minutes or until fully cooked to your liking. Just keep in mind that with the shrimp the burgers are bigger than a normal burger so may take a little more time to cook. Serve on your favorite bun and with any of your favorite toppings. This is very delicious on a potato bun or brioche bun and I enjoy it with lettuce and tomatoes and mayonnaise or a little BBQ sauce.

Creole Seafood Stuffed Red Snapper with a Jalapeno Chimichurri Sauce

Ingredients:
2 Large Whole Red Snappers
1LB Crab Claw Meat
1LB Shrimp Chopped
1 Stick Butter
1 Yellow or White Onion
1 Cup Breadcrumbs
1 Bunch Green Onions
Creole Seasoning
Garlic Powder
Salt
1 Bunch Fresh Parsley
½ Cup Olive Oil
5 Cloves Garlic minced
8 Slices of Bacon
2 Teaspoons Oregano
2-3 Jalapeno Peppers diced
1 Lemon

Method:
In a large skilled melt, the butter and add the chopped yellow or white onion and green onions as well as 3 cloves of the minced

garlic and about 1/3 or the chopped parsley (around 1/3 cup) and blend well until vegetables soften then add the chopped shrimp and crab meat and blend well. Take two strips of the bacon and fry them chopping into pieces and add to the stuffing mix. Next, slowly add the breadcrumbs and seasonings and once blended to your satisfaction (about 10 minutes) turn off the stuffing, if it's not thick enough you can always add more breadcrumbs.

Clean and wash your fish removing all the insides and washing and sprinkle with a light amount of salt, be sure there are no scales on the outside you might ask a butcher to clean the scales off for you or you can simply use a knife to remove the excess of scales. You can have the fish cut along the stomach enough so that it opens in half or just enough to fully stuff the fish with your dressing. Once both fish are stuffed fully with your dressing wrap each piece of fish with three slices of bacon and squeeze fresh lemon on the outside of both fish and wrap in foil cooking on the grill for 35-45 minutes or until done. You may also cook this in the oven on 350° for about the same amount of time but you will get a more distinct and flavorful fish if done on a charcoal grill.

Now to a blender add the remaining parsley, 2 cloves of garlic, about half a cup of olive oil, salt, and the diced jalapeno peppers (removing the seeds first). Blend well to make your chimichurri sauce. This fish goes well with a sweet white wine and a salad. Use your chimichurri sauce to dip your fish which will come right off the bone when lifted with a fork. This is a dish I grew up loving that my mom would make during football season. We only lived two blocks from the 49ers stadium, Candlestick Park, and my parents' were season ticket holders and if you know anything about tailgate parties it's all about the food! Enjoy and Go Niners!!

Epilogue

IV. Lagniappe: Evening Conaque in Cali

Gumbo Circuitry

My feet only know one way:
These generational roots and routes
Grandma's kitchen
rooted to Nanan's

It's a circuit.
A pattern.
That Spanish moss
it tells stories.
It holds memories.

Smell dat heat.
Taste it.
It's a movement.
A People.

From water to land,
from table to People,
we a Community.

We form a circuit of ancient mounds.
A People still here.

Gumbo circuitry
Every ingredient makes the magic.

But don't burn the roux.
You know we come in all colors.

A mosaic.
A pattern.
A circuit.

We thrive chér.
We thrive.

We are still here
growing roots,
making new routes,

and tracing old byways.
It's still about the People
Peoplehood.

Wi hokišak kuš.
We are all related.

AFTERWORD

Hiwéw Shokmiso Hoktiwé

Hiwéw shokmiso hoktiwé   I give thanks that we are together
Hiwéw kot nesh   Grateful for that tree
Kot nē   That land
Kot tan   That sky

Hiwéw ot hāk ya wi   Grateful for you and I
Yukiti iyeć ike awa   We rise from water
Ya awa yukiti payók   And to water we return

Yukiti comsh   We walk with support
Ike yukit okēt   From our mother
Ne naws loš   Earth help us

Hiwéw shokmiso hoktiwé   I give thanks that we are together

~Maaliyah Papillion
Bvlbancha
2024

Andrew Jolivétte, PhD: is Professor and Department Chair of Ethnic Studies as well as the inaugural founding Director of Native American and Indigenous Studies (NAIS) at UC San Diego. Dr. Jolivétte is a former Professor and Department Chair of American Indian Studies at San Francisco State University and a Senior Ford Foundation Fellow. He is the author or editor of nine books in print or forthcoming including the Lammy Award nominated, *Indian Blood: HIV and Colonial Trauma in San Francisco's Two-Spirit Community*, *Research Justice: Methodologies for Social Change* and *Louisiana Creoles: Cultural Recovery and Mixed-Race Native American Identity*.  An enrolled member of the Atakapa-Ishak Nation of SW Louisiana, he is the tribe's former tribal historian and is born of the Hiyekiti Ishak [Sunrise People] of the Tsikip/Heron Clan. He is a Louisiana Creole of Ishak, West African, French, Spanish, Italian, and Irish descent. Professor Jolivétte is the Board President of the American Indian Cultural Center of San Francisco and the Board Chair of the Institute for Democratic Education and Culture (Speak Out) as well as the co-chair of the newly formed UC Ethnic Studies Council. A former Indigenous Peoples Representative to the United Nations Forum on HIV and the Law, he is active in both scholarship and community work. Dr. Jolivétte currently serves as an Advisory Board Member with the UCLA *American Indian Culture and Research Journal,* as the Series Editor of Black Indigenous Futures and Speculations at Routledge, as a Chief Investigator with the Australian Research Council (ARC) Centre of Excellence for Indigenous Futures (CEIF), and as a Scientific Research Mentor for the IHART (Indigenous HIV/AIDS Research Training Program) at the Indigenous Wellness Research Institute (IWRI) at the University of Washington in Seattle.

Rain Prud'homme-Cranford, PhD: is a scholar-writer-singer-songwriter-musician- visual artist-thinker. Her recent books include the co-edited collection *Louisiana Creole Peoplehood: Afro-Indigeneity and Community* (University of Washington 2022)l *Miscegenation Round Dance: Poèmes Historiques* (MEP 2021), and the forthcoming *Gumbo Stories: Rhetorics and Quantum Relation-Making in the Creole South* (forthcoming). Current book projects include, *"Gather at the River": Spiritual Ecologies in Red/Black Literatures*, and *Singin' the Tides Homes: Poems in Call, Response, and Chorus*, written with her kinfolx Carolyn Dunn and Maaliyah Papillion (Bayous & Byways Books 2024). Rain works as a visual artist primarily in pen/ink, watercolor, graphite and charcoal, mural, photography, clay, and digital hand drawn paint mediums. Her art has been featured in various collections, books, book covers, and apparel and accessories. You can find her art in print, apparel, and accessories on Amazon as brand FemnBelGrasArts and at her Etsy and Tee Spring store under the same name. An Associate Professor of English and International Indigenous Studies at University of Calgary, she is a "FATtastically Queer" Louisiana Creole working primarily within Gulf Creole, Indigenous, and Afro-Indigenous Studies. She is the Executive Editor, Publisher, and Book Doula of That Painted Horse Press. Most importantly, she is a partner, Auntie, daughter, sister, cousin, an adopted mom to the two coolest kiddos ever, and an "adopted/substitute" Auntie to a flock of graduate and former students.

Andy Airey is a Canadian settler of Norse-Gaelic descent, currently living in Moh'kins'tsis where they are completing their final year of a BA in International Indigenous Studies and Global Development Studies at the University of Calgary and will start their MA in the field of political science, with the intent of contributing meaningful research to settler identity transformations on Indigenous land and in the politically-urgent era of reconciliation. A practicing pagan and animist, Andy has led many lives including a professional classical singer, an artist, parent, and sibling. Andy is committed the reclamation of intrinsic, pre-colonial culture and lifeways as an act of reciprocity to the land and its beloved peoples.

**Tracey Colson-Antee** is a Louisiana Creole/Atakapa-Ishak activist-educator and entrepreneur who has spent her life working on and with Louisiana Creole cultural education, preservation, and reclamation. She established Maven Consulting, working with non-profits, businesses, and communities to build capacity, community engagement, and development planning. Growing up in the home of a Creole cultural non-profit executive director and a Louisiana Folklife storyteller she has a unique foundation of service, pride in community, and preservation. Tracey has worked for over 25 years with various nonprofits in historical and cultural preservation, mental health, unhoused individuals and families, and population health. In addition, her passion to revive rural communities and ability to see potential and growth provides a unique perspective on addressing civic pride. An experienced Resource Matchmaker, she works with individuals and organizations to put the right pieces together to create strong partnerships and significant growth. She is a culture keeper and public speaker whose work has appeared in *Yellow Medicine Review*, *THE CREOLE BOOK*, and *Louisiana Creole Peoplehood: Afro-Indigeneity and Community*. She is currently at work on a collection of stories and memoir centering Cane River and Louisiana Creole culture.

Maaliyah Papillion is an actress, singer, model, and third-generation traiteur/ yukhiti ipošok/root-worker (healer) from a long line of traiteurs. She is a master's student in the MLS Indigenous Law program at University Oklahoma. Upon her graduation in Fall 2024, she hopes to use her knowledge to better aid her tribe, the Atakapa-Ishak Nation of SW Louisiana, in all future endeavors. A Louisiana Creole of Atakapa-Ishak and Choctaw descent, her debut poetry book  *Traiteur's Tarot: Feathers, Fledglings and Flight* (TPHP 2025) focuses on retelling her ancestors' stories in modern ways. *Singin' the Tides Home: Poems in Call, Response, and Chorus*, written with Rain Prud'homme-Cranford and Carolyn Dunn will be published by Bayous & Byways Books, winter 2024.

The Geary Hobson & Ken Jolivétte Elder and Community Stories Series:

This series honors Dr. Geary Hobson (Arkansas Quapaw/Cherokee) and the late Ken Jolivétte (Louisiana Creole/Atakapa Ishak). Dr. Hobson is the founder of the Native Writers' Circle of the Americas (NWCA) and co-founder of Returning the Gift: American Indian & Indigenous Storytelling Literary Festival (RTG), a seminal Indigenous literary studies scholar, author, mentor, and elder. Mr. Kenneth Jolivétte (1949-2022) was an esteemed and beloved Louisiana Creole culture bearer, activist, storyteller, father, and elder who centered his Creole culture while advising, inspiring, and modeling community for younger generations. This series imprint centers community, culture, family, stories, and arts from and by community leaders, elders, wisdom-keepers, and senior community members.

That Painted Horse Press (TPHP) Catalogue

Gumbo Circuitry: Poetic Routes, Gastronomic Legacies, by Andrew Jolivétte
Exile Heart: Poems, by Kim Shuck
Ope': Collected Poems, by Yulu Ewiss
Mother of Chaos Queen of the Nines, by Kelly Clayton
Toledo Rez & Other Poems, by Thomas Parrie
Texas… to get Horses, by Kimberly G Weiser

TPHP Forthcoming Titles

Tunica Stories II: Nuhchi Tahch'i Tihkarhilani (The Sun Woman's Story)/ Kaya Tayoroniku Tahalayihkuku Onti Ya'unihki (Why the Tunica and the Biloxi Became Friends)/ The Flood Myth, By The Tunica Biloxi Tribe of Louisiana, Language and Culture Revitalization Program
An Incident Every Sunday: A Novella, by Edyth Hobson
   (The Geary Hobson & Ken Jolivétte Elder Series)
Traiteur's Tarot: Feathers, Fledglings and Flight: Poems & Pictures, by Maaliyah Papillion
Soul Food, by Tonya Holy Elk
Indians, Oil, & Water: Indigenous Ecologies and Literary Resistance, (The Janet Ravare Colson Peer Review Series), edited by, Kimberly G. Wieser and Rain Prud'homme-Cranford
When Spirit Don't Rest: Haints & Horror Tales in Color, (The Janet Ravare Colson Peer Review Series), edited by, Rain Prud'homme-Cranford, and Kelly Clayton
These are the Stories: Stories & Memories, by Charmaine Shawana
   (The Geary Hobson & Ken Jolivétte Elder Series)

Anniversary Reprints Upcoming:

Outfoxing Coyote: Anniversary Edition, by Carolyn Dunn
Calling Out After Slaughter: Anniversary Edition, by M. Carmen Lane

TPHP Imprints

The Geary Hobson & Ken Jolivétte Elder Series
The Janet Ravare Colson Peer Review Series
Coyotess Books [Chapbook and Children's Imprint]

www.ingramcontent.com/pod-product-compliance
Lightning Source LLC
Chambersburg PA
CBHW070148080526
44586CB00015B/1898